WORDS OF ——————————————
INSPIRATIONS AND HOPE

WORDS OF
INSPIRATIONS AND HOPE

FROM SAI BABA

JULIET D WILKINSON

authorHOUSE®

AuthorHouse™
1663 Liberty Drive
Bloomington, IN 47403
www.authorhouse.com
Phone: 1-800-839-8640

Published by AuthorHouse   06/28/2012

ISBN: 978-1-4685-8263-5 (sc)
ISBN: 978-1-4685-8264-2 (e)

Contents

Swami's Message...i

Baba's Darshan iii

Glossary...319

About The Author...323

Swami's message

Use every little experience as a teaching tool, put out of your mind any belief in chance or accident, and know that everything that happens here down to the smallest thing is an outpouring of my limitless love and tailored especially for you. Notice the line you get into and the state of your health and body, the way you feel, watch act and look, who you meet and how, observe especially your reactions to situations.

Just as in school, some will be teaching tools, others are testing you to show you how you are doing, see the whole atmosphere as a reflection of your inner being the mandir is your heart, I dwell in it and the ashram is your identity and the village is your worldly the ashram, you have more of a chance, but it is still very easy desires, in the village you are strongly pulled outwards and away from me, in to become distracted, in the mandir(your heart) you can actually see me from time to time, but even there it is easy to be only half present and not realize that I love to give, by my grace, this outer show gives you the means to strengthen the contact to me in your heart.

Make use of your time, concentrate every iota of your attention on me open yourself totally whenever you catch a glimpse of my gown, be ready to except an out pouring of my grace at any time, what you want, ask for, and I give you, but do not expect.

Think always of those more deserving than you and know that what you receive is an act of grace and love.be open and free from fantasy and projection, just be mine and I will be yours, this way you will find happiness and fulfillment, remember that I am not only in Sai Baba from here, though that is central, but hidden embodied in everyone who is here can you find me in them or see you distracted by the outer characteristics and habits? Look deep with eyes of love and surrender your habits, yearn for me, that is my darshan which is also available, honor the many examples here. Accept my grace from whatever source it comes, be loved blessed, life with God is bliss because you surrender everything to him, do everything for him. SRI SATHYA SAI BABA

BABA'S DARSHAN

Always find a quiet corner after my darshan, where you may enter the stillness and receive the completion of my blessing.

My energy goes out from me as I pass by you, if you proceed to talk to others, immediately this precious energy is dissipated and return to me.

Rest assured that whatever my eye sees becomes visualized and transmuted, you are changed day by day, never underestimated what is being accomplished by this act of darshan.

My walking among you is a gift yearned for by the Gods of highest heaven, and here you are daily receiving this grace.

Be grateful.

These blessings you receive will express themselves in their own perfect time.

But remember that to whom much is given, from him much will be demanded.

I HAVE BEEN PRIVILEGED TO HAVE SPENT TIME IN PUTTAPARTHI. IN THE PRESENTS OF BABA, AND SHARED IN MANY DARSHANS WHILE AT THE ASHARAM!!

ALL PROCEEDS FROM THIS BOOK, GOES TO HELP THE CHILDREN OF, ST JUDES CHILDRENS HOSPITAL

JULIET D WILKINSON

God is all names, and all forms

1

If there is righteousness
in the heart, there is
harmony in character
If there is beauty in
character, there is harmony
in the home
If there is harmony in the
home, there is order in the
nation
If there is order in the
nation, there is peace in
the world.

The mind is like a lake, when the water is calm, the rays of the sun are reflected on the surface of the water, like those on a mirror, but if the water is disturbed because the wind is blowing, then there is very little reflection.

Man must learn to control his mind, man is divine and if only he could remember that, he would see life so very differently, he would cease to be affected by so much of what goes on in the world.

Difficulties are created to increase the yearning, and to sift the sincere devotee From the rest.

Men yearn for good time's high
status, power good life
But seldom do they yearn for
good thoughts, wisdom and virtue.
What better advices can
Sai Give?

The strong will is the best tonic;
The will becomes strong when
you know that you are a child
of immortality, or a person who
has earned the grace of
the lord.

The lesser the number of
your wants
The greater is your freedom
and the richer you are, the
greater the number of your
wants, the lesser is your
freedom and the poorer you are.

Instead of making the senses which are at best very poor guides and informants his servants, man has made them his master

Learn to speak little and to
speak softly
That will reduce the chances
of getting angry
Seek the good in others and the
evil in yourself.

Give up the company of the
worldly minded
The association with those
infected by evil qualities
Keep away from every type of
wrong doing
Seek always the company of
the wise, the good
Take refuge in God, he the
pure one, is the embodiment
of peace
Of happiness and knowledge.

If you live on the level of the
body, and the individual, you
will be entangled in food
Entertainment and frivolity, in
ease envy and pride.
Forget it, ignore it, overcome
it, you will have peace, joy
and calm
On the divine path, there is no
chance of failure; it is a path
on which every milestone
Is a monument for victory,
It is the path of love.

When troubles come, look beyond
the mountains to the blue skies; see
that you are witnessing my play.
See that your life is as temporary
as the dancing clouds, you're
coming and your going is just part
of your performance.
Take God alone seriously, and
play the parts you are given by me
with love, I will grieve should you
misunderstand your roles, you are
the spirit within you;
You are your blessed self; my
kingdom that is within you is your
real home.
"Oh how I love you, how I care
for you come! Rejoice with me,
you are ever dear to me."

Most devotees seek, health, wealth,
power and fame from God,
Which are trivial assets,
yielding momentary pleasures

Love as thought is truth
Love as action is righteousness
Love as feeling is peace
Love as understanding is
none—violence.

Character is the hallmark
of man, a life without good
character is a shrine without light
A coin that is counterfeit, a
kite with the string broken

Learn to speak what you feel,
and act what you speak

"*As science develops and technology advances, humility and love should also develop to the same extent*".

Let different faiths exist, let
them flourish, let the glory of
God be sung in all languages in
a variety of tunes.
Respect the differences between
the faiths and recognize them
as valid.
As long as they do not
extinguish the flame of unity.

When grief overtakes you, you run to God" when joy is restored you throw him overboard, devotion is not a temporary slave, it is the unbroken contemplation of God without any other interposing thought or feeling

The wise are those who know the self!

"Self confidence is the foundation
Self-satisfaction is the will
Self-sacrifice is the roof
Self-realization is life itself.

There is only one caste
The caste of humanity
There is only one religion
The religion of love
There is only one language
The language of the heart
There is only one God
He is omnipresent.

Start the day with love
Fill the day with love
Spend the day with love,
End the day with love

Do not cage God in a
picture frame
Do not confine him in an idol
He is all forms He is all names.

Service to man is service to God

Discipline is the weapon of growing children

Living with God is true education, living for God is true devotion, and living in God is true spirituality

I have come not to disturb, or destroy any faith, but to confirm each in his faith so that the Christian becomes a better Christian, the Muslim a better Muslim and the Hindu a better Hindu

Be convinced that God can and
will appear in any form, do
not refuse to recognize
Divinity in the form you dislike
and did not expect.

Educated man must realize that he has more obligations than privileges, more duties than rights.

Learn to adapt, adjust and accommodate.

A void pomp exhibition, and
boasting be simple, sincere and
sweet

God belongs to all
He is universal.

The mother is the pillar of the home, so of society, of the nation and so of humanity itself.

Hands that help are holier,
than lips that pray.

God is the mother and father of the world, our parents are the mother and father of this body.

What is the unmistakable mark
of a wise man? It is love, love
for all humanity.

What one meets in life is
destiny, how one meets it is
self-effort.

It is only in the depth of silence, that the voice of God can be heard.

Even death is sweeter than the bondage of ignorance.

Life is the best teacher
Nature is the best preacher.

Truth is the all protecting God; there is no mightier guardian than truth.

Faith in ourselves and faith in God, that is the secret of greatness, for God is love.

Money comes and goes;
Morality comes and grows

A sound mind ensures a sound body
A sound body ensures a sound mind.

Love lives by giving and forgiving
Self-lives by getting and forgetting

Love is selflessness
Selflessness is lovelessness

You are three people
The one you think you are—body
The one others think you are—mind
The one you really are-divine.

The peace that pervades the heart can never be shaken for any reason;
Only peace of this kind is worthy of the name.

It is not the standard of living that is important, but the manner of living.

You must render service out of
spontaneous urge from within
With a heart filled with love.

A society has to be welded into a unit by, the consciousness of kinship in God

*If one student is bad, only
that student is affected.
But if one teacher is bad,
hundreds of students get spoiled.*

Your thoughts play a vital role in shaping your life.

Reform the body, reconstruct the mind, regulate the way of living, then the country will become automatically strong and prosperous.

Forget the harm that anyone
has done to you, and forget the
good that you have done to others.

The present is a product of the past, but it is also the seed for the future.

Today's man is pursuing unrestrained sense cravings. These pursuits drag man's mind into the gutter.

The acts of Sai are always selfless sacred and beneficial.

As close as you are to God, so close God is to you

*Fire is hidden in wood and
God in man*

Every cell in the human body is God; everyone has God as the source.

When heart speaks to heart, it is love that is transmitted.

The pure heart is the inner purpose of all Saadhana.

The loot is education, and the fruit is virtue.

I am the AATMA that dwells in all living beings, I am the beginning the middle and the end of all things.

All that you see in the cosmos, the moving and the stationary objects is a manifestation of the AATMA.

Anger is the worst exhibition of the ego

One who has the true spirit of sacrifice gives to others without any hesitation or reservation. Smilingly and gladly even his dearest and highest possession.

When you feel that you cannot do good, at least desist from doing evil, that itself is meritorious service.

Just as all limbs and organs are interconnected by consciousness, so that when a thorn pricks the foot, the eyes start shedding tears, so too all countries of the world are interconnected.

So that no country or community can suffer pain, without affecting all others.

Each religion teaches man the righteous path, he has only to know it and march along
If the vision is straight, what can division do?

No religion has a separate
God, showering grace upon
those who profess to abide by
their faith alone!
It is the destiny of man to
journey from humanness to
divinity.

The whole of mankind belongs to one religion, the religion of man. For all men God is the father, as the children of one God all men are brothers.

I have come to sow the seeds of faith in God.

Buddhism:
Remember the wheel of cause
and consequence, of deed
and destiny and the wheel of
Dharma that rights them all.

Hinduism:

Listen to the primeval pranava "AUM" resounding in your heart as well as in the heart of the universe.

Christianity:
Cut the I feeling clean across
and let your ego die on the
cross, to endow on you eternity.

Zoroastrianism:
Offer all bitterness in the fire
and emerge grand, great and
Godly.

Islam:
Be like the star which never wavers from the crescent, but fixed in steady faith.

Do not give room for differences based on language, religion, caste or nationality. Develop the feeling that all are children of God.

You may worship God in any form of your choice, but always bear in mind that God is one, cultivate love and promote unity and harmony among all.

With faith man can achieve anything; faith is the foundation for the realization of God.

The world is the temple of the universal soul.

The soul does not die; only the body dies, when man knows this, death loses its sting, death is not feared.
Death is but a welcome voyage into the know harbor

More than all other forms of love,mans first efforts should be to fix his love on the lord.

Blessed are those who pray
for others, for in so doing they
become aware of the unity of
all life.

Have confidence in yourself
and strive to understand well the
nature of God's love.
To secure that love is the
sacred goal of human life.

BHAGAWAN, SRI SATHYA SAI BABA

Is the master of this house;
a silent listener in every
conversation, and unseen guest
at every meal.

There are some who live in a perpetual hullabaloo, in a tornado of noise whether they are in an exhibition or a fair, or a hotel or temple of the Prasanthi Nilayam.
They wag their tongues and will not stop; these will not proceed far on the Godward road.

Before you
TALK-THINK is it
necessary?
Is it true, is it kind, will it
hurt anyone, will it improve
upon silence.

Silence is not a matter of resolve!
It is always there, silence is
the endless flow of pure God
into you, in the world.

Know that I am always with
you, prompting you,
and guiding you.
Live always in that constant
presence.

Patience is all the strength man needs.

The purpose of living is to achieve the 'living in God'

Silence is the speech of the spiritual seeker.

Love seeks no rewards; love is its own reward.

God gave you the time space
cause material idea skill chance
and fortune
Why should you feel as if you
are the doer?

No one can judge another, for
when another is judged you are
yourself condemned.

There is no living being
without the spark of love; even
a mad man loves something or
Somebody.

So long as we do not understand that divinity exists in all, we cannot even be human, how then can we be divine?

Only in fear of sin can you experience peace and non-violence.

Knowledge without action is useless, action without knowledge is foolishness.

Make the mind the servant of GOD, not the slave of senses.

Your body is the temple of GOD.

Laziness is rust and dust;
realization is rest and best.

Anger is like a intoxicant; it reduces the man and degrades him to the level of an animal.

God is simple everything else is complex.

However high you may rise in social status, however huge may be your bank account, if your parents are neglected in distress; your life has been a tragic waste.

Do not get attached to worldly things and pursuits, be in the world but do not let the world be in you.

You are all members of the same family, bound by the religion of love.

Do not seek to discover the evil in others, for the attempt will tarnish your own minds.

True education is not for a mere living, but for a fuller meaningful life.

Devotion is not a uniform to be worn on certain days, and then to be put aside.

Self is the base of foundation
Help is the wall
God is the roof of the building
Light is the owner.

The mind is a bundle of desires, remove the thread of attachment one by one; at the end the "cloth" disappears and the mind is clear and pure.

PRACTICE SILENCE:
For the voice of God can be
heard in the region of your
heart, only when the tongue is
stilled and the storm is stilled,
and the waves are calm.

SPIRITUAL EXERCISES;

"The more intensity, the greater the results".

Practice the vocabulary of love;
unlearn the language of hate
and contempt.

Life is a challenge, meet it!
Life is a dream, realize!
Life is a game, play it!
Life is love, enjoy it!

If the mind of man is not reformed and purified, then all the plans to reform the world will be futile.

Whenever and wherever you put yourself in touch with God that is the state of meditation

What God gives is never exhausted,
what man gives never last.

The soul is not the object of intellect; it is the very source and spring of intellect.

The gift of food to the hungry is the noblest of all gifts.

Mankind can find happiness only in unity, not in diversity.

WE MUST CONTROL OUR DESIRES

Do not waste money

Do not waste time

Do not waste food

Do not waste energy

Real peace of mind has no ups and downs; it cannot be partial in adversity and whole in prosperity.

Love sees all as one divine family.

Thinking discriminating and practice, all three constitute the basic human characteristics.

Soft sweet speech is the expression of genuine love.

Reason can prevail only when arguments are advanced, without the whipping up of sound.

Education should build character.

Character is to be sought more than intellect.

It is truth and truth alone,
that is one's real friend,
relative

What is the unmistakable mark
of a wise man? It is love, love
for all humanity.

Love does not allow any room for pettiness or narrow outlook.

The teacher of tomorrow, are the students of today.

Knowledge without devotion to God, produces hatred.

You must welcome test, because it gives confidence and it ensures promotion.

Always respect another's opinion and another's point of view.

If you honor your mother,
the mother of the universe will
guard you against harm.

If you honor your father, the father of all beings will guard you.

*If you honor
your parents,
your children will honor you.*

When the magnet does not attract the needle, the fault lies in the dirt that covers up the needle.

Have faith in yourself, when you have no faith in the wave, how can you get faith in the ocean?

Your thoughts, words and deeds will shape others, and theirs will shape you.

The end of knowledge is love; the end of education is character.

Each country is but a room, in the mansion of God.

*Nourish your aged parents,
revere them.*

The very joy derived from service, reacts on the body and makes you free from disease.

The age period 16-30 is
a crucial stage, when man
achieves best and struggles
hardest to achieve.

The mother is the pillar of the home, of society, of the nation, and so of humanity itself.

To reform, first weed out the evil thoughts and bad habits, second cultivate good habits.

Peace it can only come from the fountain of peace within.

Man loves, because he is love,
he seeks joy, for he is joy.
He thirsts for God; for he is
composed of God and he cannot
exist without him.

Either the Government must have the capacity to educate and reform the people or the people must have the capacity to educate the government.

By peace, western countries mean
the interval between two wars.
That is no peace!
When man thinks, speaks and
does good peace will ensure.

Where there is love, there God is evident.

Seeing is believing; I will believe in God only if I see him; but are all things seen or heard or touched or tasted, as real as they seem?

Do not preach; practice

It is best to live with honor
for just a day, than with
dishonor for many decades;
better a short lived celestial
swan, than a century lived crow.

Do all acts as offering to God;
do not classify some as "my
work" and some as "his work"

The honor of a nation depends on the morality of that nation.

God is the life breath of every soul.

Nothing is to be used as itself for itself.

The beauty of life depends upon our good habits.

Life is a mirage; it comes from
no visible rain, it falls into no
recognizable sea.

Love expands; it does not limit itself to boundaries.

Do not contemplate on death;
it is just an incident in life,
contemplate on God, who is the
master of all life.

Detachment is sacrifice.

GOD first
The world next;
Myself last!

All things in creation are subject to the law of change, and man too is subject to this law.

Example, not precept, is the best teaching aid.

Service is spiritual discipline, not a pastime of the rich and well placed.

Real happiness lies within you.

Too much food results in dullness of mind.

God alone is the giver of life,
the guardian of life, and the
goal of life.

Spirituality is an activity; it is an activity of the divinity within.

Base all educational efforts
on building up the character of
the students, and then you can
confidently think of raising
on it the super structure of
curricula.

Man is the spark of the divine.

Where there is faith, there is love.
Where there is love, there is peace
Where there is peace there is
God And where there is God
there is bliss.

All spiritual practice must be directed to the removal of the husk, and the revelation of the kernel.

You cannot see me, but I am
the light you see by
You cannot hear me, but I
am the sound you hear by
You cannot know me, but I
am the truth by which you live.

The same current activates all.

The whole world is one single
tree, the different countries are
its branches, its root is God.
Human beings are the
flowers, happiness is the fruit,
self-realization is the sweet
juice therein.

All works is God's, he inspires, he helps, he executes, he enjoys, he is pleased, he reaps, he sowed.

*Jesus renounced everything,
to become fit for service to
mankind.*

One single act of service
offered to God, whom you
visualize in another is worth all
the years of yearning for God.

Spiritual progress is right living, good conduct, and moral behaviour.

Speak soft and sweet, sympathize with suffering and loss and ignorance, try your best to apply the salve of soothing words and timely succor.

The greatest fear man can have, is the fear of losing God's love.

The eternal has no birth and death, no beginning, no middle nor end;
It does not die, it is not born, it can never be destroyed; it is the witness,
The self, the Aatma;

Make the home a seat of harmony.

God is the mother and father of the world, our parents are the mother and father of this body.

Discipline is the mark of intelligent living.

Mine not thine, this sense of greed is the root of evil. This distinction is applied even to God, my God not yours! Your God not mine!

The goal is one, for all roads must lead to the one God.

You may be able to pay back any debt; but the debt you owe your mother, you never can repay.

If you know the road and the goal, then you can discover whether you are progressing or not.

*Be loving, begin to perceive
your inner voice and follow it.*

You must be a lotus unfolding its petals, when the sun rises in the sky. Unaffected by the slush where it is born, or even the water which sustains it!

Do not use poisonous words against anyone, for words wound more fatally than even arrows.

Love knows no fear, and so love needs no falsehood to support it.

Do not belittle any religion, or give predominance to any single religion.

Implant in your heart;
Do not forget God; do not
put faith in the world you see
around you, do not be afraid.

The wise are those who know the self.

Truth has no fear; untruth shivers at every shadow.

Each man carries his destiny in his own hands.

Dreams relating to God are real.

Sensory pleasures are trinkets, trivialities

God is the doer; you are but the instrument.

If some people say there is no God, it only means they are at too great a distance to be aware of him.

Man seeks to change the foods
available in nature to suit
his tastes, thereby putting an
end to the very essence of life
contained in them.

Be simple and sincere.

Our good conduct is our true wealth.

Resolve to carry on the quest,
of your own reality.

Duty without love is deplorable;
Duty with love is desirable
Love without duty is divine.

The easiest way to control sensuous desires is to practice altruistic love.

Hatred sprouts, envy raises
its hood.
Love sprouts, peace descends
like dew.

The day when passion is accepted as a mark of womanhood, it will mark the beginning of the end of feminity.

Live on your own earnings, your own resources.

Cultivate that attitude of oneness between men of all creeds, all countries and all continents.

God is omnipotent all powerful, God is omnispresent, present everywhere. God is omniscient all knowing.

Activity must be dedicated to God, the highest good, then it will provide health to body and mind.

Love with no expectation of return.

Do not waste a single moment,
in idling or loose living.

If you feel you are a hundred per cent dependent on God, he will look after you and save you from harm and injury.

Love of country is the basis on which you can build love for the world.

*If you safeguard righteousness,
it will in its turn, safeguard us.*

Discipline trains you to put up with disappointments; every rose has its thorn.

There may be differences among men, in physical strength, financial status, intellectual acumen, but all are equal in the eye of God.

When you retire for the night,
offer grateful homage to God,
for being with you all day long.

Aspire now, adore now,
achieve now.

Have the name and form of
God as your companion, guide,
and guardian, throughout the
toils of the waking hours.

Self-mastery
Campaign against the temptations of the senses; conquer inner foes, triumph over your ego.

Practice alone makes man perfect.

Life is the car, your heart is the key, God is the chauffeur.

God is not to be spoken of as coming down or going up, since he is everywhere.

To rectify the world and put it on the proper path, we have to first rectify ourselves and conduct.

Man can realize his mission on the earth, only when he knows himself as divine, and when he reveres all others as divine.

Teachers are reservoirs from which, through the process of education, students draw the water of life.

Knowledge that is not put into practice is like food that is not digested.

It is easy to conquer anger through love, attachment through reasoning, falsehood through truth, bad through good and greed through charity.

Look upon joy and grief as teachers of hardihood and balance, grief is a friendly reminder, a good taskmaster; even a better teacher than joy. God gives both protection and punishment; for how can he be the lord if he does not insist on strict accounting and strict obedience?

There is in this world no austerity higher than fortitude, no happiness greater than contentment, no punya (good deed) holier than mercy, no weapon more effective than patience.

Ego gets and forgets, love gives and forgives.

I am aware of why you suffer, and how you can escape suffering.

It is part of human nature
that man desires to reach the
presence of the almighty, to see
him and be ever with him, for
deep within the human heart
is the urge to reach the place
from which he has come.
To attain the joy he has lost,
the glory which he has lost, the
glory which he has missed.
Man is himself divine and so it
is a matter of the deep calling
unto the deep, of the part
calling for the whole.

The lord does not weigh the status or caste of an individual, before bestowing his grace. He is all merciful and his grace falls like rain, or moonlight on all the people.

God is neither distant nor distinct from you.

You will understand me only through my work, that is why sometimes in order to reveal who I am, I myself show you my visiting card, something that you call a miracle.

Falsehood looks easy and profitable, but it binds you and pushes you into perdition.

Freedom is independence from externals, perfect freedom is not given to any man on earth, lesser the number of wants, the greater is the freedom, hence perfect freedom is absolute desirelessness.

The moment you realize that you are not the body, that very instant all the attachments and delusions will disappear.

Gain inner peace, inner joy; that can be done only when you act without an eye on the gain. The act must be its own reward; or rather the act must be according to the prompting of God within, so that its consequence is left to him. Practice this attitude consistently, and you will find great peace welling within you and around you.

Cleanse your mind of the temptations and tenets of ignorance; make it free from dust, so that God may be reflected therein.

Give each problem the attention
it deserves, but do not allow it
to overpower you.

Anxiety will not solve any
difficulty, coolness comes from
detachment, above all believe in
God and efficacy of prayer.

The lord has said that he
who does good, thinks good and
speaks good will not come to
harm.

That is the way to get
equanimity, shaanthi.

The secret of liberation lies not in the mystic formula that is whispered in the ear and rotated on the rosary.
It lies in the stepping out into action, the walking forward in practice.

*God has come in human form
and move about among them, so
that he can be
Listened to, contacted, loved,
revered, and obeyed.*

Why fear when I am here,
have faith that SAI is with
you at all times and all places.

*Truth is more fundamental
than an atom.*

You are in the light, the light is in you, you are the light.

Love not lust is the essence of a happy life.

Love is my form, truth is
my breath,
My life is my message;
expansion is my life
No reason for love, no season
for love, no birth, no death

Spirit can only be awakened
and realized through individual
discipline and the grace of God.
These two can be won through
love, purity and service to others.

Past is past, it can't be recalled future, you are not sure of, the given moment is now.

PRESENT

This present is omnipresent.

You heart should be filled
with compassion towards all
living beings.
You should fill the suffering
hearts with prema. (Love)
You should radiate thoughts
that can generate aananda
(blissful peace)

Prayer must emanate from the heart, where God resides, and not from the head where doctrines and doubts clash. Prayer has great efficacy, the Vedic seers' prayer for the peace and happiness of all mankind, of all animate and inanimate things.
Cultivate that universal vision.

The feeling of friendship must activate every nerve, permeate every blood cell, and purify every emotional wave.

It has no place for the slightest trace of egoism, you cannot elevate the companionship which seeks to exploit or fleece for personal benefit, into the noble Quality of friendship, perhaps the only friend who can pass this rigorous test is God.

After long searches, here and
there, in temples and in churches,
in earths and in heaven, at last
you come back, completing the
circle from where you started.
To your own soul, and find
that he whom you have been
seeking all over the world, for
whom you have been weeping
and praying, in churches and
temples on whom
you were looking as the mystery
of all mysteries, shrouded in the
clouds in the nearest of the near,
is your own self, the reality of
your life body and soul.

Believe firmly that the body is the residence of God, that the food you eat is the offering you make to your deity; that the bath you take is the ceremonial bathing of the divine spirit in you.

The ground you walk upon is his domain, the joy you derive is his gift, the grief you experience is his lesson that you tread the path more carefully.

Remember him ever, in sun and shade, day and night, awake or asleep.

Love you religion, so that you practice it with greater faith, and when each one practices his religion with faith, there can be no hatred in the world, for all religions are built on universal love.

Be attached under all conditions
to the source, substance and
sum total of all the power
The Lord, then you can draw
from that source all that you
need. This attachment is called
BHAKTI.

To discover ones reality and to dwell in the divine peace, one need not give up the world and take to asceticism

You must come to me for a Darshan to fill your heart with joy and ask forgiveness

The Darshan enables you to recharge your mental battery when it becomes weak.

Individual effort and divine
grace are interdependent,
without effort; there will be no
conferment of grace.
There can be no gain from the
effort, to win grace you need only
to have faith and virtue.
Knock the doors of grace will
open, open the door, the sun's
rays waiting outside will flow
in and fill the room with light.

An evil eye sees evil in others.

The human being is a composite
of man and beast and God.
And in the inevitable struggle
among the three for ascendency,
you must ensure that God wins.
Suppressing the merely human
and the lowly beast.

Removal of immorality, is the only way to immortality

Brahma was in existence, well before mind and intelligence came into existence.
Brahma cannot be understood by one's mind or intelligence.

No one has a right to advise others, unless he is already practicing what he preaches.

Science is below the mind,
spirituality is beyond the mind.

Hardship keeps one always
alert and trim; they reveal
hidden resources of skill and
intelligence.
They toughen fortitude and
deepen the roots of faith.

The message of the fatherhood
of God and the brotherhood
of man, which Jesus Christ
proclaimed two thousand years
ago, should become a living
faith for the achievement of
real peace and the unity of
mankind.

The oneness of creation,
affirmed by the ancient seers
and sages, can only be expressed
in a transcendental love which
embraces all people, regardless
of creed, community, or
language.

See God installed in everyone:
everybody is a temple.
Where the omnipresent God is
to be adored and worshipped by
your service.

A pure though from a pure heart is better than a mantra.

I am always guarding you and guiding you, march on, have no fear.

*No person can dream of
Swami, unless Swami himself
desires it so.*

To eliminate the ego, strength
the belief that all objects belong
to God and you are holding them
on trust.
This would prevent pride; it is
also the truth.

You might have heard people
talk of the miracles of my
making, this and giving that,
of my fulfilling your wants.
Of my curing your illness, of
course I confer on you these boons
of health and prosperity, but
only so that you might with
greater enthusiasm and with
less interruption, proceed with
spiritual saadhana.

Dedication is different from service, in service there is the element of ego, "I serve He is the master, he acquires my service for him, I am necessary for him.

But in dedication, the I is wiped out, there is no desire for the fruit; the joy consists in the act being done.

To cultivate that attitude of dedication, everyone must think of God, remember the name of God and deepen faith in God.

To achieve release, man kneels
before a million Gods, in
frantic pain.
If he blasts the ego within,
the goal is reached, he is freed
indeed.

Everyone is eager to be happy,
everyone thinks that wanting
more and working less to
earn the things wanted, is the
quickest way to be happy,
no one tries the other method,
wanting less and working more.

The real and the unreal are not two distinct things, one is the absence of the other, that is all, there is only one appearing as two, the pure mind reflects the reality clearly-God, that is the basic of self as well as the objective world.

God is immanent in every particle in the universe.
The clear vision can experience him everywhere at all times, and that vision confers immeasurable inexpressible bliss.

Politics without principles
Education without character
Science without humanity and
commerce without morality, are
not only unless, but positively
dangerous.

God of death does not give
notice of his arrival to take
hold of you.
He is not like the
photographer who says,
"I am clicking are you
ready?"

Let the wave of memory, the storm of desire, the fire of emotion; pass through without affecting your equanimity.

Small minds select narrow roads; expand your mental vision and take to the broad road of helpfulness, compassion and service.

Women have equal chances and equal rights to attain Godhead.

Once we surrender our minds to God completely, he will take care of us in every way.

Love is the scarcest article today!

The heart of man, which is now allowed toile fallow, has to be plowed by spiritual Exercises like repetition of God's name.

Philosophy that cannot be
understood, scriptures that are
not practiced
The present world has plenty
of these
It is a waste to talk of them

I AM
"SATHYASYA
SATHYAM"
THE
"TRUTH OF
TRUTHS"

GLOSSARY

Om	THE PRIMAL SOUND A-U-M
AVATAR	AN INCARNATION
AANANDA	DIVINE BLISS-ETERNAL BLISS
INDRIYA	SENSES
BHAKTI	DEVOTION TO GOD; INTENSE SELFLESS LOVE FOR GOD
BHAKTA	A DEVOTEE WHO HAS INTENSE LOVE FOR GOD
SAADHANA	SPIRITUAL DISCIPLINE OR EFFORT AIMED AT GOOD REALISATION
AATMA}	SELF; SOUL, SELF, WITH LIMITATION, IS JEEVA (THE INDIVIDUAL
SOUL)}	SOUL) SELF, WITH NO LIMITATIONS, IS BRAHMA (THE `SUPREME REALITY)
SHAANTI	PEACE

PREMA	ECSTATIC LOVE OF GOD ; (DIVINE LOVE OF THE MOST INTENSE KIND)
PUNYA	VIRTUOUS DEED
BRAHMA	THA CREATOR; FIRST OF THE HINDU TRINITY
SATHYAM	TRUTH
SHIVAM	GOODNESS, AUSPICIOUSNESS
SUNDARAM	BEAUTY
SADHU	A GOOD PERSON-DETACHED VIRTUOUS AND WISE
NAMASMARANA	REMEMBERING GOD THROUGH THE NAME
SEVA	SERVICE
DHARMA	RIGHTEOUSNESS, DUTY
MANDIR	TEMPLE
SANKARA	THE FIRST PHILOSOPHER OF ADVAITHA
BUDDHI	INTELLIGENCE
SATHYA	SAI SAI BABA'S NAME-ALSO MEANS TRUTH
SADHAKA	A SPIRITUAL ASPIRANT
NARAYANA	GOD

SWAMI   THE WAY SAI BABA IS
         ADDRESSED, IT MEANS THE
         LORD AND MASTER

ABOUT THE AUTHOR

JULIET DELIA'ANN WILKINSON

BERMUDIAN

JULIET, HAS TRAVELLED ALL OVER THE
WORLD SEEKING SPIRITUAL KNOWLEDGE AND
GUIDANCE!!

AND HAD THE PRIVILEGE OF HAVING VISTIED,
SATHYA SAI BABA,BEFORE HIS ASCENSION!!

PLEASE NOTE THAT ALL PROCEEDS FROM THIS
BOOK, WILL GO TO HELP THE CHILDREN OF
ST JUDES CHILDRENS HOSPITAL.

JULIET

"ALSO FOR THOSE PEOPLE WHO HAVE
HAD THE PHENOMENAL EXPERIENCE,OF

RECURRING DREAMS,AND ACTUALLY SEE
THEM MANIFEST"

A MUST READ BOOK!

HIS EMINENCE ABUNA YESEHAQ MANDEFRO,
JULIET & BOB MARLEY.

BY JULIET